To
Marguerite
Happy reading!
Love from Beth – your – fellow – poet!

Essential Journey

Harbour Poets

GW00640748

First Edition 2009

ISBN 9780955060557

Cover image
© Sarah Pearce 2009

Design and Layout by
Sarah Pearce, Lou Brown and Ged Duncan

Set in Georgia

Published by Bardic Media Ltd
2 Hardy Cottages, School Lane
West Lulworth, Wareham, Dorset BH20 5SA

Printed and bound by Copytech (UK) Ltd
Peterborough

www.bardicmedia.co.uk

www.harbourpoets.info

" There is energy and honesty in the language of the Harbour poets and they know how to use it well. Here carefully crafted phrases capture the smell of summer and the feel of a Weymouth winter. History and heartache are discovered in a tin of molasses and in stories from the graveyard.

And there is also a wonderful, vibrant variety. Poems written with gentle good humour play with words and ideas and others, with angry precision, scythe through hypocrisy. Grockles visit Uranus and we learn the art of listening while elsewhere the cost of war is counted out to a relentless rhythm.

This is the work of skilled craftsmen and women who don't allow us to see the effort that goes into catching moments and emotions. This is a journey worth sharing: this is a journey to remember."

Bridget Whelan.
Author of 'A Good Confession.'
(Severn House)

Harbour Poets
Essential Journey

On an icy February day, schools, universities, offices, shops and councils across the UK were closed due to heavy snowfall, and the public were urged to venture out only if their journey was absolutely necessary.

Later that day there was a well-attended gathering of the Harbour Poets.

All agreed that Poetry was an Essential Journey.

Harbour Poets is based in Weymouth, Dorset. The group was founded early in the 1990's and has met continuously ever since. It has an open membership and poets meet to read and discuss their own work in a friendly and supportive way. All abilities are welcome – the group has had members ranging from beginners to a Bridport Prize winner. The only membership criteria are a liking of a warm drink and good company...and a poet's soul.

www.harbourpoets.info

Essential Journey

Contents

Frank Alcock

"His poetry is that of a craftsman. Each and every word has the importance of musical notation and the result, with sensitivity and delicacy of touch, is work of both significance and substance." (John Kemp)
Frank's most recent collection is 'The Fiery Eye.' (Piscean Press)

The Summerhouse

In the summerhouse we talked
of the next twenty years of happiness,
in gardens heady with flowers, walking
through evenings of long sunsets.

In the summerhouse the white-ribbed
roof arched delicately over
us where we sat, silent
in the still garden, after sunset.

Waiting for death or rebirth
we welcomed the dawn
with wide-eyed surprise.
Remembering, then, yesterday's worth
as a day to celebrate or mourn,
in a summerhouse white like lies.

Perhaps

Alone she steps, unawares.
A slim, black figure,
black hair curled
close to her neck,
white fingers clenched
as she steps lightly over
rocks at the sea's edge.

At rest on a rock, bowed
like a black question-mark
begging an answer:

elbow on knee, hand
cupped to her chin, face
turned to distance as eyes
scan seas for a sign,
a clue to the enigma
of her baffled heart, her
Self.
  Perhaps, alone
with her pain, she'll see
the answer to her question,
her body sheathed in black
top, black jeans,
white face framed
in black.
  Perhaps, the white
flame of her question will light
the answer at the dark heart
of her adolescent quest –
imperative as her sex,
undeniable as death.

'Heavy Plant Crossing'

Heavy plant crossing: bold, flamboyant, unbending?
Having blundered out of Time, blinded by white space;
Triffid tons, stomping reverberating road;
Or soundlessly slithering, tentacular, silently screaming?

But not green – no! Absurd to believe
It burgeoned monstrously in dull, ubiquitous green –
How disappointing! Venusian blue, palpitating?
Or Martian red, three metres flowering, beautifully

Horrendous? Or black, menacing and slimy! Why not?
Who's ever seen heavy plant – crossing or not?
Perhaps, arrange a rendezvous, at moonlit crossroads
With the curious: assorted weapons glinting wickedly.

Rain

Rain ceases; insinuates itself
In sensitive shapes of tremulous calm;
Lies, idly, enclosing the sky,
Mirroring blackness of floating branches,
Primeval limbs in illusory depths
Of long-sunken, sedimentary light.

Only this cherry tree has colour:
Its red blossom flaring, like severed
Nerve-endings, flourishing its pain;
Plunging inwards in a stasis of drowning,
Deep down the looking- glass sky
To a world where daylight's unknown;
Where strictures of time are in abeyance,
Where there is, perhaps, a sense of peace.

Continually, such images are lost
In sunshine or deluge, unaware of our loss;
Continually we sail, in frailest of coracles,
Unreflective, in the mirror of the rain, on our loss.

On the Beach

The light is bright, so bright
and sea an iridescence of child's eyes,
and beach a miscellany of treasures
picked up by inquisitive fingers,
and waves quickening his feet in the foam
as he jumps in and out of the tide.
Paddling in the sea – this man
happy as the day forever -
playing out his time till the last
twinkling of the sun so bright.

Later, darkness and sleep -
As if light and brightness had never been -
but, wrestling through a sea of dreams
he hears a child calling, calling,
a child beckoning him back
to yesterday, and play forever
on a faraway beach, in a twinkling sun.

Weymouth Bay: Winter

A spangle of lights, night ships' glow:
Holiday yachts or floating casinos?
The wavy line of the tide reaches
A subtle conclusion, enhancing the beach.

This risky glitter of lights promises adventure -
Gambling and tippling, a tinkling music?
The tide's white finger daringly reaches
A wild conclusion, disturbing the beach.

Lovers, in silhouette, idle along the sand:
Passionate, or serene, hand in hand?
The tide's white edge cleanly reaches
A flourishing conclusion, defining the beach.

The ships' lights shine, a stoical burning;
The lovers. Fading, vanish – consumed with yearning?
The white tide, eternally turning, reaches
Another beginning over the cold beach.

Elsa Corbluth

*A founder member of Harbour Poets, Elsa has lived in West Dorset for
45 years. She has published three main poetry collections, 'St. Patrick's
Night' (Peterloo), 'The Planet Iceland' (Peterloo) and 'The Hill Speaks'
(Jurassic Press). She has won some national and international poetry
prizes. These three poems are from 'The Planet Iceland.'*

Song of The Oil War

I am the oil-blacked bird of war.
My neck is slicked with national greed.
My flight is checked on tar-caked shore.
My life is left where dark oil bleeds.

I am the water's weighted chest.
I am the oil-choked lungs of air.
I am the earth's oil-wounded breast
And human cities past repair.

I am the faceless face of war
Burned out of life while sheltering.
I am the oil-teared child of war
And families past comforting.

I am the oily tongues of men
Whose oily language fills each home
Of those who wait in dread and pain.
I am the powerless and the dumb.

I am the surgical attacks
Played on a screen, the firework show.
If "friendly fire" precision lacks
I'll justify those deaths, I know.

I am the oil-bright eyes that kill
And oil-dark eyes in their defeat.
I am the victory that still
Guns down an army in retreat.

I am the weapon traders' gain
With no care where my weapons sell
Though on my neighbours' sons they rain.
I am the bank accounts of hell.

I am the sun cold as the moon,
A skull of light, the night in day.
I am the liberateds' boon –
To face a summer, chill, oil-grey.

I am the medieval plagues
That follow clean computer wars.
I bring starvation. Mine's the vague
Belief, it was a worthwhile cause.

I am the desert of the heart.
I am the desert of the mind,
War's end that is the next war's start.
I am the desert of mankind.

Spells

She speaks in whispers as though listening
for the soft approach of elf companions.
Hildur, tapestry artist,
weaves wools of stone shades, sky and sea gradations
and muted lava mauve, dull rose and charcoal.
The river lights her room. In the brief summer
she paints her roof rich blue. In autumn, kneeling
on grey-green moss threaded with gold and scarlet
miniature trees, she picks the indigo berries.
In the extended winter, in day-darkness,
she walks the river's ice to the lit town
under the pale green swirl of northern lights.

She knows elves watch her from their snow-fleeced hollows
along the banks. One comes into her kitchen,
a tall and moss-grey woman elf and sits there,
fluid like a shadow.

> In that sparsely-peopled country,
climbing alone, I wonder if they've trailed me,
hovered between me and my foolishness,
guided me along that snow-melt ridge
that sucked like quicksand, put my wobbling feet
on miles of stepping stones, showed me the one way down,
by brittle rock holds, from the wave-point edge.

Once, with an arm-swing, did they ring me round
with a rainbow, overhead and underfoot,
I standing on a rock, midstream, the basalt rods
of the waterfall above, fine mist below,
encircled, centred in a rainbow?

> Did they creep
behind me up the July winter gully
to where I hesitated at the steep iced snow,
put in my hand a broken-off spade handle
I then used like an ice-axe to the top?

Did they, by any chance, go hand in hand
with my son, stamping the sharp lava scree
to the last summit of Kristínartindar,
I crunching close behind? Did they throw wide
a blue glass sky and the immense white sweep
of Vatnajökull? Did they make us hear
that prickling stillness, and, at long still intervals,
were they the ones to – drip – that single stone?

Swan Man

"This bird is one hundred per cent truth
Can you say that of a friend?"
She is faithful for life to one.
It is only the fishing lead,
Mistaken for innocent stone,
Will take her from her mate
To him, her healing man.

As the swan visited Leda
The man came to this swan.
Bending to her like a myth
He works in wing-shadow,
Her neck a tall flower stalk
Wilted in half on his hand.

Under the wing of night,
Forgetting his woman-mate,
His family and home,
The man is tending his swan,
His warm solicitous hands
Running the length of her neck
Which holds the killing stone.

In the wood-river smell of his shed
And the spell of the spotlight moon
The man is her only one.
In their backwater ballet,
On her rumpled liquid bed,
Two massed white cyclamens,
They flower into one swan.

The lead is one hundred per cent lie:
Death of the bird in her throat.
The man is one hundred per cent life
In the shed of her silver night.
In his house on the curve of the bank
His woman and children lie
While he stands with his swan by the slats
Of moon-white in case she should die.

If she lives he must carry her back
To her mate who drifts like one
White water-lily: he must let them bloom,
While he turns, with his man's feet, home,
Who cannot, in the morning, stay a swan.

John Kemp

John's poetry is largely pastoral, using the natural world around us as a metaphor for whatever meaning he wishes to convey. He likes to think that his work is accessible, lilting and musical, reflective of shared experience. Thus there is a touch of melancholy and loss, leavened with hope. John's most recent collection is 'Music of the Day' (Woth Press)

Blackberry Camp

There is nothing here
but beech and mound
and songbird sound
with a wind from the west
scratching at the thorn
while underfoot fallen leaves
whisper as one passes
as mourners might
to one who grieves.
No name survives,
no face. The grasses
on the banks
sway in silent ranks
to quiet music of the day,
breeze and bird, and sheep
deep in Southleigh Combe
this lambing time.
Those people would have heard
sounds similar to this
and doubtless thought
upon its lovely transience
and said, maybe, in tones
as casual as that passing crow,
face to grubby face,
others shall be happy here,
like us, yet leave no trace.

Quenched Fire

The Axe had broadened
to an estuarial display
of greys and silvers,
of pewter hammered on by
currents, vagaries and sun,
was travelled on by winds,
leaving dying wakes and ripples
and transient tracks as clear
as those that oyster catchers
leave on mud; so many birds
were there, low tide, slack
water, all along the edges
probing thin cries into salted
air. A boat approached on
bright reflecting wings
and all the sea birds took
to sudden flight and with them
went, as though they carried
all away in one whole sheet,
the estuary entire; and what
remained was a wooden boat
on wooden water and silence
like that of a quenched fire.

I Owe You

Were you ever found seated
and sated, contented,
idly gazing at sky
with little to do but enjoy,
hill farmer, as idle and sated
as now sit I?

... whatever your giving
    your living was meagre
    but good to the eye,

the shaley grey walling
rising and falling
that insatiable hill
gives the lie.

I owe you, my masters,
Harnessed to callus and stone,
I owe you my ease,
But you lie under headstones
Unheeding, unneedful,
Where now in the autumn
Fall soundless the leaves.

In Their Season

With fingers curled
round cups of tea
and walking sticks beside,
we sip at tables on the Esplanade
and watch incuriously
the rising tide;
behind the hunched and quiet town
the hills in late October brown,
impassive seem in autumn dream,
murmured on by bees
and soothed by drifting thistledown,
but underneath the furzy heath
silent under cirrus skies,
colder grow the roots below
as each in fading season
every system dies.

Sometimes A Rose

Where this lane bends
then dips and turns again,
a stream runs. It has a name
I usually forget. Yet
when I come upon it
it is always the same; there
is a scent in it, summer
or winter, no matter. The dip
-because the air lingers there,
I suppose- harbours a
scented stillness as though it remembers
honeysuckle and hay and sometimes
a rose.

Self Heal

Foxglove, mullein, wall rue, clover
with wild bees over, jackdaw, rook,
south wind soothing waving grass,
the grass running now to seed: blackbird
in the copper beech and the tower
ringing the quarters of each hour
high above the churchyard where
the gravestones lean. Daisies,
love in the mist, lavender. Silence,
then at three the peal. Buttercups,
and written on stone "Thy will be done"
Ants on the wall. Self heal. Sun.

Eve Devenish-Meares

Eve was Born in Beccles, Suffolk, of a Lancashire father and a Yorkshire mother, and encouraged to read poetry from an early age. Her mother came second in the Woman's Hour Poetry Competition in 1956. Her daughter Ann chose a poem for the children's choice book "I like this Poem" in 1979. Now it is her turn.

Generation Gap

Children can't be trained to sing your song
Another generation leads their way
They take a path to which you don't belong.

Nourish them and try to make them strong
Cherish and hope but tell them what you may
Children can't be trained to sing your song.

Lead as you think their lives should go along
They will watch others, follow trails they lay
They take a path to which you don't belong.

Tell if you think that they are going wrong
But they're not hearing anything you say
Children can't be trained to hear your song.

You wish perhaps your children less headstrong
So for close ties, for love you only pray
They take a path to which you don't belong.

While in your heart their stay you would prolong
Another calls them and they may not stay
Children can't be trained to sing your song
They take a path to which you don't belong.

Our Garden

Our garden is small and limited
A tiny pond and a bush or two
Yet my view is varied everyday
By visiting pairs of passing birds.

Two magpies come and sit on the roof
Or splash in the pond, one at a time
Two crows aggressively drive them off
When the bird table beckons with food.

Another day when the sun is bright
Two doves may appear to own the place
They coo and bow and generally court
Along the edge of the garden fence.

The sparrows visit in more than twos
Sometimes a single robin appears
But then two blackbirds come for a dip
And we are back to normal two by two.

There's a time of year when ducks appear
A change from squatting in the creek,
They take up a stance at the top of the roof
Surveying our world with complete delight.

Picnic

Take a baguette of bread
Some delectable cheese
A bunch of grapes and
A peach would please.
With a litre of wine
To drink at your ease
Oo- la- la fast French food.

August

The roaring thinder rolls aross the world
As lightning flash illuminates the sheep
The dog, distracted, roams restlessly about
And heat prevents a long and restful sleep.

The farmer will be glad he laboured on
To gather up and roll and packaged hay
But in our streaming garden, rain collects
The grass may not be cut again today.

Hippopotamus

H is name was Humphrey, he lived in the mud
I n a wide shallow river, quite close by the
P ub, with nine other friends he would wallow and
P lay, blowing sometimes lying doggo all day.
O n his back in the sun two small birds would bide,
P ecking, busily tweaking, grooming his hide.
O n the top of his head there were two hard bumps
T wo little ears flicking when the birds took jumps.
A lways brightly alert, tiny eyes watchful
M outh opening W I D E to receive any morsel,
U psetting, this habit, for the drunk that he
S wallowed, in the mud, just close by the pub.

Rainbow

R adiant smiles on faces shine
A s arcs of colour paint the skies
I n the mix of rain and fine.
N one who pause to raise their eyes
B ehold the bow, earth crowned by line
O bserve with wonder, thinking, wise,
W alk on untouched by heaven's sign.

Friendship

F avourite companions are the ones who treat you best
R eal listeners who share with you and choose you from the rest
I n the happy times and hard times
E ven if their trust is tried
N ot needing reassurance, near at hand or far and wide.
D uring partings, in an absence
S haring life through thought and prayer
H appy in the memory and knowledge they are there;
I n hopeful expectation of meeting as before
P roposing now and always to be friends for ever more.

England

E veryone comes to England now
N o better place to be, they think
G lory days have passed away
L ords and Ladies talents hidden
A nd anyone may try their luck
N o one needs an education, but
D aring to live and work takes pluck.

Banana

B abies' mash with sugar and cream
A n adults fritter-in-brandy dream
N oon snack or after dinner split
A thletes, walkers fuelling kit
N umbers of uses whatever the mood
A curvy tube of instant food.

Barbara Davis

Having lived in Norfolk, Hertfordshire, Hong Kong, Sussex, South Wales and Dorset, Barbara's poems have evolved from her experiences gained over 60 years, intermingled with a sense of humour and an inherent love of poetry. She goes to bed with a different poet every night.
(On CD of course!)

Rotational Impostation

If the Hadron Collider
Produced a microscopic
Black hole as predicted
It probably wouldn't matter.
For like Alice's Tea Party
With the Mad Hatter.
It would exist for only
A moment in time,
For about a nano-nano-nanosecond.
What could possibly matter?
To matter in no time at all
Would our universe be sucked in?
Turned inside out like a large sock
Would the dormouse awake?
In his tea-pot
To find himself
In an alternative galaxy
Where white dwarfs and neutron stars dance
Over the tablecloth
Forming and re-forming –
Cups – plates and teapots.
Shapes changing as cosmic rays collide
All rotating, held together by string theory
A black hole of uncertainty
As to what is real
And who is the impostor at the party?

Saint's Feet

I have always desired feet like a Saint's
With long thin bones, shell nails to paint
A lady Chiropodist once told me true
Your feet are beautiful, they work for you
No fragile metatarsus or ballerina arch
Like a cart-horse, your feet are made to march
Squarely across the furrows of life
Your feet will carry you, causing no strife
For they are square and flat, solid the bone
Firmly planted in Earth's good loam.

'Your toes are the same length' my husband would greet
'Ten little chipolatas on the end of your feet
This piggy went to market and this stayed at home
Imagine them frying, lovely and fat - little bone!'
Then came my ankles, oh! deary me!
Less than willowy, more like stumps of a tree
Socks never stayed up, rumpling would curl down
Elastic tops digging purple welts all around -
My leg, so I would stretch and pull at the top
Bemoaning who ever made awfully thin socks

Then I'd get my scissors, what a sin!
I'd start to snip around my shin
First at the front, but alas still too tight
So I'd snip some more, oh! what a sight!
A shaggy top, crenellated castle walls
Will my trousers cover this fringe that appalls?
As I gaze down with heavy heart
I know my feet can't be called 'art!'
No Saint's feet heeled with Angel's Wings
But I can truly say 'THEY'RE BEYOND THE FRINGE'

Cynheidre Dust
(for Alan – a Miner)

Orange dust in the flickering light,
Amber droplets coursing down streaked torso,
Muscles bunched, straining to hew the coal
From the earth's deep deposits.
Machines grind relentlessly
Churning chunks of anthracite.
Dust swirling in continuous eddies,
Creeping inside cuffs and collars,
Gritting 'the snap', furring the tongue.
Conveyor belts thrum through miles of tunnels,
Nosing up through levels like blind moles,
Reaching the open air depositing vast black cones,
Pile upon pile of ancient fossilized forests.
Tired men, shift ending, file into the lamp room,
Lights dowsed, helmet upon helmet line the shelves.
Canaries sleep in their cages,
Each pick cleaned, laid ready for the next shift.
Stripping off overalls,
Men file into the communal showers,
Like Black and White Minstrels
Bodies pale alabaster, hands and faces coal engrained,
Lifted to the steaming shower,
Voices raised in song,
Backs lathered, scrubbed by buddy,
Until last in line steps out,
Towelling roughly, hastily dressing –
Now to down a pint at the club,
Antiseptic against the dust
Beer, lubricating, sluicing over clogged tissues,
A toast to the black gold.

Under The Bridge

"What is your wish?" he said,
"To go under the bridge," she said,
"Go get your boots, we will meet on the beach"
Which was small, busy with ropes and nets.

The jetty clanked, clear water seeped through rusted grid,
The boat nudged alongside, engine thrumming –
A working fishing vessel – She perched tentatively
In the bows, his form filled the tiny cabin.

Revving the throttle they moved away into space,
Like a rocket ship crossing the vastness of sea and sky,
So diminutive in the great blue expanse, neck craning
Upward at the container ship anchored at rest in the bay.

Passing through the gap in the harbour wall
The wind pulled and lifted,
Her body rolled with the motion,
Familiar landmarks seen afresh across the sparkling waves.

Turning into the harbour she could have trailed her hand
In their bubbling wake, part of the mariners' world,
Passing moored vessels, waving to the Lifeboat crew,
The bridge loomed in front of them.

The tide was high; he manoeuvred the bows back -
Until she was 'Under the Bridge' in its dark coolness,
The echo of feet above, the heavy movement of vehicles,
The pumping of her blood as swift as the tidal flow.

Looking up she could see the crack where she always crossed.
The join in the bridge where she jumped and wished,
Now she was here 'Under the Bridge' –
What to wish for next?

Robin Daglish

Robin is a semi-retired builder and has lived in Weymouth for ten years.
The T.E.Lawrence poem 'to S.A'. in the Seven Pillars of Wisdom inspired
him to start writing. Fifteen years later he's written hundreds of poems
and have been published in Orbis, South and others.

St Catherine's Chapel

He was born on a flat earth
Stretched on the rack of the sky and sea,
Taught to fear from birth
The hellfires of eternity.

His breath was built of prayer,
His body an ache for the spirit's rise,
His death a doorway, not despair,
Purification at the bodies demise.

Because he was human, because he had sinned,
He cut stone from Chilsden hill,
Stacked it against the devil's wind.
Cemented it with stubborn will.

With a jealous God to please
He strained with blistered hands,
Till the sun had dropped to its knees
Over these monastery lands.

He built a stone altar
On a green pedestal hill,
So that he would not falter
Till his weary heart was still.

The chapel was built and the sun sank
The captured sea harboured the moon,
By the footstool of a pebble bank,
At the swans neck of the long lagoon.

Weymouth Harbour 11am

The half-time score is one all
to the sun and rain.
As the sky changes ends
I descend the rain-silvered steps,
squinting through the broadside
of reflected light from the ferry.

Along the harbour a woman hunches
over her long lens, fishing for images
among the bright boats.
She ignores the false horizon of black hills
dumping rain on distant cliffs,
focuses on the pristine lifeboat
afloat on a broken mirror:
a shoal of light.

The Balcony

Out there in the punishment of air,
Fortuneswell is stacked against the steep hill,
Traffic labours up in low gear to where
Seagulls patrol broken-nosed cliffs.

The angle grinder is sending
Sparklers flying, a galaxy of stars
Falling to earth, descending
A ladder of light.

I cut away the rust and rotten wood
That has not withstood the west wind.
There's scaffolding where people stood,
A skywalk to be underpinned,

Cantilevered out over slates
And crooked chimney stacks
That wear their pots like jaunty hats,
Taunting the sea below.

Light thickens in the late afternoon,
Shadows brew in bay,
Distant sounds become more hollow:
It's time to put the tools away.

Insurance Claim

These millions of cars can't keep avoiding one another.
My foot slipped off the clutch and hence
a face like a car wreck was surveying his rear bumper.
He told me he had just customised, at huge expense,
his pride and joy: a mark two zodiac.

He opened the boot and I saw
straight through to tarmac:
a coastline of rust, edged a vanished floor;
a rusty exhaust pipe, repaired with an old tin can
and a wired up silencer, dangled to the ground.

This was just the start of his plan:
of course his engine had seized, he found
that the big end had gone and his camshaft
had suffered whiplash and ripped out all the trim,
and he'd have to claim for his divorce – he laughed,
because his wife had just left him.

Why don't you take my house and all my savings?
I said, that should compensate your strife,
and to alleviate your sufferings
I can let you have my wife.

Weymouth Gasholder

Behind the harbour of idle masts
a mighty diameter sits on its nest of pipes:
anchored anachronism,
complacent in its riveted volume.

They'll knock it down one day
and build flats
but for now the old stub stands its ground:
a round tower repelling boarders,
an eyesore, a spoilt view.

In mitigation I would ask for a lesser sentence.
I love the way it has rejected grey:
in rusting tastefully it has the aura
of a permanent sunset.

The Nothe Fort

Pug ugly on its promontory,
a pugilist in stone,
fugitive from glory,
isolated and alone.

No fripperies or Rapunzel towers,
no princesses here,
just heavy gun emplacements,
blood, sweat and tears.

Now it's a seaside spectacle,
a curiosity by the sea:
museum of defence
that helped to keep us free.

Richard Green

"A member of Harbour Poets since 1995, in that time Richard has written over 200 poems emphasizing his own unique lateral thinking. Like rockets, the poems can dazzle you with humour used to illustrate a more serious undertone. On reading his work you may wish he were published more widely." (Barbara Davis)

Interstellar Tourist

The Solar System?
Oh! We only made a flying visit,
A Tuesday afternoon, I think.
It rained.

Pluto we had to miss "Closed
For re-decoration." Neptune
Glimpsed in the distance
Was weird, blue and spooky.
As for Uranus! You couldn't move
For grockles, with their plastic macs,
Sticks of rock, candyfloss, kiss-me-quick- hats
And crates of warm brown ale.

At Saturn though, we had super fun
Scooter race, three times round the rings
And last one back to the spaceship
Does the washing-up.

Jupiter was a gas
We all got giggly and rather high
At a surprise
Bring a cylinder helium party.

Mars? I don't remember Mars
Ah! Yes, that was where
We went on a romantic
Double moonlight canal ride and I
Must admit I rather fancied our hunky gondolier

With his metallic arms and legs
Square green head, radar aerial ears
And sexy X-ray eyes.

The next planet?
No, we steered well clear
You see, we'd read the signs
"Danger – Keep Away
Don't Go Near. Radiation Zone
All life extinct."

Saint George

picture me at breakfast, just an ordinary
knight in shining armour, I had no idea
this day was to be anything special
as I munched my wholemeal toast and crunched
my snap-crack-popping cornflakes

looking for a crusade to join
I chanced upon a nearby town
(attracted by the racket)
the harassed ratepayers
were ringing their bells and praying
one of their princesses
kidnapped
"almost a virgin," they declared

assuming a devil-may-care air
we clip-clopped out to meet the monster –
breathing fire he stood foursquare
over the comatose girl, proud of his trophy
but knowing he had stepped out of line
broken the contract whereby creatures of myth
and sensible parents who don't believe in fairies
can exist side by side – as opposition
he must have thought me rather poor;
a preliminary test to soften him up for the hard men
or, maybe a bizarre joke
at my feet, he seems

much smaller, no longer a threat
his nostrils gently smouldering – pathetic
it's not yet 11 o'clock and already
I'm a hero forever

the princess over my shoulder, warm
softly breathing, how sexy she seems –
aware, now, of my place in history
I **don't** stop in the woods and have my wicked way
though that's not
what I'll tell the lads, when drunk on cheap wine
we next meet to swap
stories of slaughter and rape

cheerful citizens line the walls –
now it was safe, a posse of their bravest
ventured out to greet us; the council
passed a resolution asking me
to stay and be married, but I,
making light of my escapade
refused money and with my horse watered
rode out of town
into the gloomy dusk

tired, my mind returns
to the momentous events of mid-morning
recalling how, when time
came to strike, I flinched,
closed my eyes, lashed out wildly,
expecting death as burning breath
seared across
my visored face

how stranger still
my hand passed through fire
and came out unscathed, and
a dragon was laid low
by a glancing blow
that scarcely scratched
its scaly skin.

The Unwelcome Guest

"I hope I haven't arrived
in the middle of your dinner"
he said as he stepped out
of the shepherds pie and
knocked over the salt.
Carefully removing the peas from his ears
and the carrots from his hair
he jumped down off the table
and made himself comfortable
(on top of the squealing cat)
in the leather armchair by the fire.

The Berkshire Alligator

A year ago, or so
A group of friends, swimming in the Thames
Were sure they saw an alligator
Downstream, heading for Reading.

At great expense, the Ministry of Defence
Flew over an alligator expert
All the way from the Everglades.
Armed to the teeth with harpoons and switchblades
He did nothing but complain
About the rainy climate, the waste of his time
And the lumpiness of his hotel bed.

One morning, he put on his diving suit
Tied lead weights to his size-twelve feet
Venturing to brave the murky waters
To hunt for the fearsome beast
Before he plunged into the swirling river
He shook his helmeted head
"There are no alligators in Berkshire," he said

That was the last thing he said.

Vanessa Young

Vanessa left working life in London for Dorset in 2004. She found moorings with Harbour Poets, and an inlet for her poetry in the monthly Chesil magazine for villages local to the Fleet. Recently she has been putting her own lyrics to music.

Reticent Dining

Would you think me very rude
If I preferred my solitude
And when you ask me out to dine
Say yet again, 'Another time,'
And though I love a wine rosé
And more, to share a glass with you,
Perhaps we'll meet another day
If that's what you would like to do?

June, I awaited You

June, I awaited you so long
And yet you take your leave
so soon, and leave me
trying to rhyme a song
beneath the sweet
mid-summer moon
And I must wait
another year for you
to orchestrate
the tune

Lay-by

Daisies that grow low
Keep their heads
When mowers mow

Great Preparations

From Thomas Hardy's short story
Tradition of Eighteen Hundred and Four

Old Solomon said, and I
was long alive when he was dead,
that at his shepherd father's bidding
he'd take his turn, and mend the ewes' undoing,
as spring brought after fearsome weathers
light more mild, and he
a hand at lambing, still a child.

So with the moon well travelled in her arc,
together with his father's brother, Job
on visit from the nearby soldiers' camp,
high on the downs, up over yonder cove,
they took their turn along the ancient way
to heed the bleating calls for arms,
and settled in the fold.

Soon after they had nestled in the straw
and hearing Job through laboured nostrils snore,
young Solomon, his senses still intact,
was mulling over stories of attack,
of battles fought in France and wounds run deep,
when he was roused to foreign sounds hard by,
and cautioned from his sleep
he marshalled ear and eye.

In truth, this story may make your blood curdle,
for what the boy saw on a slanting hurdle, was
two men rolling out a naval map
comparing local inlets, this with that.
Their preparations: French strategic planning;
One tipped his hat to cool his face by fanning.
You may have guessed the witness to this act
saw Boney standing there! Imagine that.

No sooner had young Solomon woke Job
and whispered what to you has now been told,
these Gallic men on board did sail away
across the Channel from our own slipway.
The pair saw all from high up on the hill
and understanding it, feared England's ill.

Job left the boy, and hastened back to camp,
and gave report and all by that was meant.
But all the serving officers could think
was that the soldier Job had taken drink.
Those preparations, at a peak that day,
were later thwarted on Trafalgar Day.

Passing By
A simple survey

    Have you been to Havant?
     I haven't.
    I bet you wish you had?
    It doesn't sound too bad.
    Have *you* been to Havant?
     I wish I hadn't!
    And you! Have you been there?
     I couldn't swear
     that I've been even near.
    Have you been?
     To Havant? If that's
     the place you mean,
     I've never been.
    Oh Havant! A place so dear!
    Yet, have I been?
    I haven't.

If a Tree Be Company
With respect to William Barnes, the Dorset poet
If a tree be company
I wonder if you could
Excuse me for a while
So I may visit once again
The wood down yonder lane
Where one is waiting tall and true,
Firm and full of grace
And old as any yew,
With outstretched arms
To welcome in embrace
As well as any fellow
John or Tom might do.
So do not sigh
If I slip out to walk nearby
Away from our concern
To where the leaves I know
Fall prey to go where
Passing winds do blow
While I, content mid earth and fern,
May sit beneath the canopy
Its heritage to learn.

Still Life

Some things a poem
Cannot convey
A cabbage resting
On a lattice plate
Green glazed, ornate
Composed, sedate
A painter this perfection
Better could relate
But my artist's eye
Bid I a poem try

Ged Duncan

Ged is sometimes to be found in a cabin in Dorset, sometimes in a garret in Brighton - seeking the middle path between plump yokel and emaciated artist. He is the author of the 'Sydney the Smuggler' trilogy. www.gedduncan.info

Listening to Frogs

I listened to Governor Plum
and he explained to me, in micro-technicality
his macro-economic theory and that money
did buy love as well as make the world go round.
I listened to Archbishop Glum
who methodically explained to me
his systematic theology and that his God
did not move mysteriously at all.
I listened to Professor Tweedledum
and he waved his hands in a particular way,
explained to me his quantum
Theory of Everything.

I listened to the sixty moons of Saturn,
sitting in the darkness of their back-scattered light
asking nothing.
I listened to this tiny spiral galaxy tucked
in a quiet corner of the universe
heard nothing, rested in her loosely-wound arms.
I listened to the universe expanding,
spun through superclusters of a trillion galaxies,
weaved through matter and anti-matter -
waited in silence at the boundaries of space and time.

I listened to a frog in a pond
and he blinked his small, round eyes
croaked noisily - told me how well
he understood the ocean.

Edges Soften

Down the long, roofed road where the dark ens
and esses entwine above me,
edges soften with a lime-green spring-sheen
which reminds me to forget
the darkness past.
Where a blackbird curtains her nest in bindweed
and exhausted martins re-render their homes
Ten thousand miles. Ten thousand miles?
Why do we do it?
Where roe deer tread dirt into bright bluebell carpets,
and humans hammer their sheds
and talk again.
Where a sheep rolls on her back to dislodge a tick,
kicks her legs like the child whose
bloat she listens for,

I put my fingers in the soil again
take the seeds and push them deep

Barrage

Straight lines are broken by darkness, dissolute
long-haired grass and unwise thistles
not yet ready to nod their grey heads.
I'm breeze-blown, night-time sat
hutside, watching with an open ear.

A feline shape, with white underside, snake-creeping
along the fence, towards the box
where birdbaby meal slumbers -
hears my hiss, the pebble-flung noise
snarls, leaps away from my missile.

Rising, radio voices from the house below
reach me through a phantom silence -
lives lost, another wartime barrage coming
- no sign of peace, despite the drowsy
light from curtained windows.

Step inside my cabin, pull the door, touch
the naked wood my hands laid there
and lie there, naked, bare, pull the blankets over.
Nothing to hear now but wind and breath
breathing itself.

Out there in the darkness
the hunter hunts, the barrage
begins again.

Moored in the Wilderness

the river's amniotic
fluid cradles me
in sleep
here
in this
curved womb

suddenly
I'm born into
the darkness
a bittern's
boom heralding
wakefulness

Dance in the dawn

Sun rises over the water,
throws the valley into shadow.
Did a pagan priest dance in the dawn
now reddening the sky?
Did we sing with him our hopes to her
that they should climb as surely upwards
- a glorious arc across the sky?

Every living thing, whose eyes
observed your rise and fall,
rose and fell like you.

Blessed are the Dead (who die in the Lord)

Maple tree shades the marble tomb
Rebecca Linette Davis, born 1922, died 1976
Dry dead leaves twisted
From twigs by the cool wind
One drifts over the fence
To the supermarket car park
One lands on the muddle of a soaking wet
Sleeping bag curled around the tree base
One circles into the cavity left
By the broken cross
Of Robert Upperton Esquire
Born 1797, died 1876

A flint wall, a flint church
When flint was harvested from the fields
Like corn
When people fled inland from the French
When there were only fifty seven people
In this place where the buses rumble past
And trolley wheels rattle urgently towards cars

Children's voices mix with the sounds
Ending day-care in the new hall
Brick beside the flint
Small hands hold hurrying well-dressed
Parents, who push their buggies past the gravestones
Past the fence dividing consecration from commerce

Beneath the tree, beside the bag is a book, fanned out and soaked
Like wallpaper waiting for hanging
A black plastic bag holds the last possessions
Of a sleeping man
Now departed.

Barry Tempest

Barry is now retired from full-time work teaching English to, at different times, secondary, further education, and degree level students. Born and brought up in Yorkshire, long-settled in Dorset, he has always, since school days, looked to a wider world, an interest reflected in many poems.

Rutupiae-Richborough

Sea, a ruined arch, an everyday
farm-gate: a brutal road
brought death along this way

when sandalled legionaries strode,
a future nestling in each soldier's sheath,
Back the other way, beyond the broad,

stone arch of creeping empire, beneath
the fronting wall of crumbling cliff, across
the straitened, wine-dark seethe

of waves, back to Gaul and Rome where all roads cross,
on to Athens, Babylon and Ur;
a myth of Eden; loss

of Africa, to Olduvai, our sore,
raw bones on our old, ancestral seat.
A single nationality is poor:

what tramps to us, the beat
of time and boots along this way,
where provenance and destinations meet!

Molasses

Dark, scalding froth turned cold
in alchemy of industry;
base become guineas, pure gold.

Sweat in black hair, heat on black skin,
mixed with the ooze from a whip;
salt rusted steel in the links of a chain:

an exchange for land over sea,
where a girl with fair hair
talks, sweetens her tea,

and those with the girl resent,
as they chew with a curious smile,
the chain that links to this present.

The Lamps of Melilla

We are the shadows in your night.
Outside the sparkles of your barbed-wire fence
we peer, your beacon

drawing us. Sense holds back;
we dare not flutter
against your flames like moths.

Dark encloses us, our loss
of your bright lights our grief.
We turn again to churning waters,

the ambiguities of shipwreck,
the coin-flipped toss of chance.
Your lamps' glow is our constant lure

on the trek to Agadir,
to leaky wood on East Atlantic waves,
the dark, dark deep.

Marabout Barracks

You easily unpick the original shape,
the parade ground edge,
the loopholes in the walls.

We use it now for civil things.
The rusty name reverberates
of Aboukir, Khartoum, the Nile way in

to Africa. The castellated gateway
is now its own museum, the flag idling
with the colours of an old imperium.

The Pity Of It
Suggested by a 1915 Thomas Hardy poem of the same title

The spring sun specks the grass
in a dell of wintry trees.
It could be anywhere in Europe.
It is Dorset. Smoke
from Thomas Hardy's wood-edge cottage
drifts beyond the beech trees.

It is Belgium. At Langemark
the sun-specks light the names
on flat black marble slabs.
German infantry lie sixteen deep,
cut down. Bare branches shield them.
The four dark watchers watch.

It is where our stories take us;
where Sigurd slew the dragon,
licked his blood-bespattered hand
and heard the wood-bird's words,
the burden understood, singing of
his folly in the gore of the speckled glade.

Requiem XX CENT

They are laid gently,
because they mattered once;
do now, to those who wait.

Those who wait have questions
that these piles of bones,
these skulls with holes,

will not answer. If the jaws
would speak, spent breath reveal
through broken teeth

the facts... did they
know, perhaps, the face
behind the finger on the trigger?

Was this a specially intimate kill,
or just a mass elimination?
Grains of earth make no distinction.

One had paused in his garden
beside a rare fig, had plucked,
and eaten, before they took him out.

Digging years later where a fig-tree grew,
they traced in its twisting roots the space
where the undigested seed had clenched his gut,

and found the bones. It is a job
done, well done, since necessary;
not finished yet.

*Suggested in part by "Bones don't speak" by Angelique Chrisafis
Guardian G2, 15-04-2008.*

Elizabeth James

Elizabeth lives in Dorset. She joined Harbour Poets in 2005 and says they have inspired her love of poetry. She likes writing about nature and the countryside. Her mother has told her that she is a country girl at heart.

Seasons

I see Easter sunshine as new life appears
I see yellow daffodils and purple crocuses,
Black and white woolly lambs frolicking
In the spring-green meadows.
Tight new buds appear on the branches of the trees,
Showing pink-tipped and cream blossoms.

I feel the warmth of summer sun on my skin
People walk along the sea front,
A young couple stop and embrace and
Old people slowly stroll hand in hand.
The cliffs gleam white in the warm sunlight.
Overhead, noisy gulls screech and dive across the bay.

I scuff through golden-brown and russet autumn leaves
As they slowly fall to the ground.
I feel the cold chill of change blowing through my life
As surely as the seasons turn.
I sense that my life is continuing to change, as do the seasons.

When cold winter creeps into my life with storms of doubt
I feel so alone and battered by lifes' problems.
Slowly a ray of sunshine comes into view,
Breaking through the black storm clouds.
Then I feel as if the hand of a friend is reaching out to me....
Someone who cares.... and peace comes once more.

Walk In The Park

High above the Nothe Park
I see the fluffy silver-edged clouds
scudding across the pale blue sky.
Deep pink and creamy white blossoms unfurling
on the swaying branches
of tall wind blown trees.

A timid grey squirrel
startled by my footsteps,
scampers over the tufted grass.
People sitting in the warm sunshine
watch the pigeons as they scratch and
peck for food along the pathways edge.

I looked at the people sharing time together.
Around me I felt the presence of nature's harmony
And was glad to be part of this peaceful scene.

Seascape

I smell the tang of seaweed on the air.
Rocks grey and black tumble down to the restless sea.
The white-tipped waves rush into shore
to grind solid stone into rough sand.

Is this the same water that saw the beginning of the
historic Jurassic Coast? With its awesome rock
formations frozen in time and the amazing fossils
set forever in stone.

Below the sea wall I hear the laughter of children as they
search for the sea-life in the rock pools, catching
crabs and shrimps in nets and being amazed at what
they had discovered on this sunny afternoon.

A Navaho Lament

I am Running Water, my people are Navaho –
the proud inhabitants of the green plains.
The silver river sparkles as it runs through the land.
It gives refreshment to our horses,
fresh life to the gold and yellow maize.

I am sitting with my sisters near our tepees.
New life grows in my rounded belly.
Talk of many strange men has reached my ears.
They have pale faces – their wooden wagons roll
with noisy wheels, over the Great Spirit's land.

There are sudden screams of terror.
Pale Faces appear with burning torches.
Cries of pain, confusion,– the wind fans the hungry flames.
All my people scatter, my sisters have all gone.
I run from the ashes of my home, to the
Pine-scented forest – Home of Brother Wolf.

I live in my allotted enclosed space on this
bleak reservation – put to one side by white men.
I ponder their foreign ways – parleys with my father –
Then – the fertile land, given by the Great Spirit
was taken away by them – for Soulless Gold.

My people are ripped apart – but my heart is still free.
It can soar with the eagles in the bright azure of the heavens.
I can remember the soft feel of Mother Earth in the springtime.
I will teach my son, the most hard – fought battles are in the soul.
He will be strong – proud to bear the name of **NAVAHO.**

www.harbourpoets.info